# What's in this book

This book belongs to

_____

# 新邻居 The new neighbour

## 学习内容 Contents

### 沟通 Communication

说出月份和日期
Say the months
and dates

数一至三十一
Count from one
to 31

### 生词 New words

| | | | | | |
|---|---|---|---|---|---|
| ★ | 一月 | January | ★ | 十月 | October |
| ★ | 二月 | February | ★ | 十一月 | November |
| ★ | 三月 | March | ★ | 十二月 | December |
| ★ | 四月 | April | ★ | 月 | month, moon |
| ★ | 五月 | May | ★ | 日 | date, day |
| ★ | 六月 | June | | 燕子 | swallow |
| ★ | 七月 | July | | 来 | to come |
| ★ | 八月 | August | | 回来 | to come back |
| ★ | 九月 | September | | | |

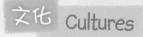

四月四日，燕子来我们家了。

The swallows came to our home on 4 April.

文化 Cultures

中国农历

Chinese lunar calendar

跨学科学习  Project

制作月历，并说出日期

Make a calendar and say the dates

# Get ready

**1**  What is in the tree?

**2**  What is it for?

**3**  Have you seen a real one before?

sì yuè
四月

四月四日，燕子来我们
家了。

六月九日，小燕子学会
飞了。

十月八日，燕子不见了。

燕子回家了，明年再来。

十一月、十二月……
燕子快回来！

四月又到了，燕子回来了！

# Let's think

**1** Recall the story and number the pictures in order. Write in Chinese.

**2** Discuss with your friend.

What does Dad say when the swallows fly away?

Where have the swallows gone?

# New words

**1** Learn the new words.

月

三月

日

燕子

来

回来

| Sun | Mon | Tue | Wed | Thur | Fri | Sat |
|------|------|------|------|------|------|------|
| | | 一 | 二 | 三 | 四 | 五 |
| 六 | 七 | 八 | 九 | 十 | 十一 | 十二 |
| 十三 | 十四 | 十五 | 十六 | 十七 | 十八 | 十九 |
| 二十 | 二十一 | 二十二 | 二十三 | 二十四 | 二十五 | 二十六 |
| 二十七 | 二十八 | 二十九 | 三十 | 三十一 | | |

**2** When are these festivals? Circle the correct answers.

1

a 六月
b 十月
c 十二月

2

a 一日
b 十五日
c 二十日

**1** Listen and colour the eggs.

**2** Look at the pictures. Listen to th

...ory and say.

十月

| 二 | 三 | 四 | 五 | 六 |
|---|---|---|---|---|
|  |  | 1 | 2 | 3 |
| 6 | 7 | 8 | 9 | 10 |
|  | 14 | (15) | 16 | 17 |
|  | 21 | 22 | 23 | 24 |
| 27 |  | 29 | 30 | 31 |

十月十五日，
爸爸回来。

我回来了！

 **3** Listen and circle the correct answers.

1 When does Mum come home?

a

四月
**16**

b
四月
**1**

2 When does Hao Hao go to school?

a

九月
**13**

b

九月
**20**

# Task

Colour the months according to the instructions. Say the months in each colour group.

一月、三月、五月、七月、八月、十月、十二月

四月、六月、九月、十一月

二月

| 一月 | | | | | | |
|---|---|---|---|---|---|---|
| 日 | 一 | 二 | 三 | 四 | 五 | 六 |
| | | | | | 1 | 2 |
| 3 | 4 | 5 | 6 | 7 | 8 | 9 |
| 10 | 11 | 12 | 13 | 14 | 15 | 16 |
| 17 | 18 | 19 | 20 | 21 | 22 | 23 |
| 24 | 25 | 26 | 27 | 28 | 29 | 30 |
| 31 | | | | | | |

| 二月 | | | | | | |
|---|---|---|---|---|---|---|
| 日 | 一 | 二 | 三 | 四 | 五 | 六 |
| | 1 | 2 | 3 | 4 | 5 | 6 |
| 7 | 8 | 9 | 10 | 11 | 12 | 13 |
| 14 | 15 | 16 | 17 | 18 | 19 | 20 |
| 21 | 22 | 23 | 24 | 25 | 26 | 27 |
| 28 | 29 | | | | | |

| 三月 | | | | | | |
|---|---|---|---|---|---|---|
| 日 | 一 | 二 | 三 | 四 | 五 | 六 |
| | 1 | 2 | 3 | 4 | 5 | |
| 6 | 7 | 8 | 9 | 10 | 11 | 12 |
| 13 | 14 | 15 | 16 | 17 | 18 | 19 |
| 20 | 21 | 22 | 23 | 24 | 25 | 26 |
| 27 | 28 | 29 | 30 | 31 | | |

| 四月 | | | | | | |
|---|---|---|---|---|---|---|
| 日 | 一 | 二 | 三 | 四 | 五 | 六 |
| | | | | | 1 | 2 |
| 3 | 4 | 5 | 6 | 7 | 8 | 9 |
| 10 | 11 | 12 | 13 | 14 | 15 | 16 |
| 17 | 18 | 19 | 20 | 21 | 22 | 23 |
| 24 | 25 | 26 | 27 | 28 | 29 | 30 |

| 五月 | | | | | | |
|---|---|---|---|---|---|---|
| 日 | 一 | 二 | 三 | 四 | 五 | 六 |
| 1 | 2 | 3 | 4 | 5 | 6 | 7 |
| 8 | 9 | 10 | 11 | 12 | 13 | 14 |
| 15 | 16 | 17 | 18 | 19 | 20 | 21 |
| 22 | 23 | 24 | 25 | 26 | 27 | 28 |
| 29 | 30 | 31 | | | | |

| 六月 | | | | | | |
|---|---|---|---|---|---|---|
| 日 | 一 | 二 | 三 | 四 | 五 | 六 |
| | | | 1 | 2 | 3 | 4 |
| 5 | 6 | 7 | 8 | 9 | 10 | 11 |
| 12 | 13 | 14 | 15 | 16 | 17 | 18 |
| 19 | 20 | 21 | 22 | 23 | 24 | 25 |
| 26 | 27 | 28 | 29 | 30 | | |

| 七月 | | | | | | |
|---|---|---|---|---|---|---|
| 日 | 一 | 二 | 三 | 四 | 五 | 六 |
| | | | | | 1 | 2 |
| 3 | 4 | 5 | 6 | 7 | 8 | 9 |
| 10 | 11 | 12 | 13 | 14 | 15 | 16 |
| 17 | 18 | 19 | 20 | 21 | 22 | 23 |
| 24 | 25 | 26 | 27 | 28 | 29 | 30 |
| 31 | | | | | | |

| 八月 | | | | | | |
|---|---|---|---|---|---|---|
| 日 | 一 | 二 | 三 | 四 | 五 | 六 |
| | 1 | 2 | 3 | 4 | 5 | 6 |
| 7 | 8 | 9 | 10 | 11 | 12 | 13 |
| 14 | 15 | 16 | 17 | 18 | 19 | 20 |
| 21 | 22 | 23 | 24 | 25 | 26 | 27 |
| 28 | 29 | 30 | 31 | | | |

| 九月 | | | | | | |
|---|---|---|---|---|---|---|
| 日 | 一 | 二 | 三 | 四 | 五 | 六 |
| | | | | 1 | 2 | 3 |
| 4 | 5 | 6 | 7 | 8 | 9 | 10 |
| 11 | 12 | 13 | 14 | 15 | 16 | 17 |
| 18 | 19 | 20 | 21 | 22 | 23 | 24 |
| 25 | 26 | 27 | 28 | 29 | 30 | |

| 十月 | | | | | | |
|---|---|---|---|---|---|---|
| 日 | 一 | 二 | 三 | 四 | 五 | 六 |
| | | | | | | 1 |
| 2 | 3 | 4 | 5 | 6 | 7 | 8 |
| 9 | 10 | 11 | 12 | 13 | 14 | 15 |
| 16 | 17 | 18 | 19 | 20 | 21 | 22 |
| 23 | 24 | 25 | 26 | 27 | 28 | 29 |
| 30 | 31 | | | | | |

| 十一月 | | | | | | |
|---|---|---|---|---|---|---|
| 日 | 一 | 二 | 三 | 四 | 五 | 六 |
| | | 1 | 2 | 3 | 4 | 5 |
| 6 | 7 | 8 | 9 | 10 | 11 | 12 |
| 13 | 14 | 15 | 16 | 17 | 18 | 19 |
| 20 | 21 | 22 | 23 | 24 | 25 | 26 |
| 27 | 28 | 29 | 30 | | | |

| 十二月 | | | | | | |
|---|---|---|---|---|---|---|
| 日 | 一 | 二 | 三 | 四 | 五 | 六 |
| | | | | 1 | 2 | 3 |
| 4 | 5 | 6 | 7 | 8 | 9 | 10 |
| 11 | 12 | 13 | 14 | 15 | 16 | 17 |
| 18 | 19 | 20 | 21 | 22 | 23 | 24 |
| 25 | 26 | 27 | 28 | 29 | 30 | 31 |

# Game

Find out your friends' birthdays and write them down. Colour the balloon.

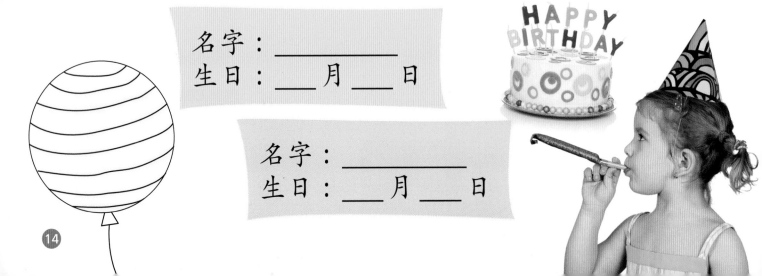

名字：＿＿＿＿＿＿

生日：＿＿月＿＿日

名字：＿＿＿＿＿＿

生日：＿＿月＿＿日

# Song

一月二月三四月，
五月六月七八月，
九月十月十一月，
十二月后又一月。

## 课堂用语 Classroom language

知道吗？
Do you know?

明白吗？
Do you understand?

做完了吗？
Have you finished?

**1** Learn and trace the stroke.

横折钩

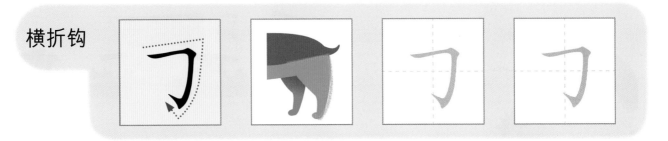

**2** Learn the component. Circle 月 in the characters.

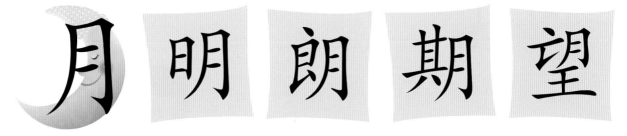

月　明　朗　期　望

**3** Chang'e lives on the moon. Colour her home.

**4** Trace and write the character.

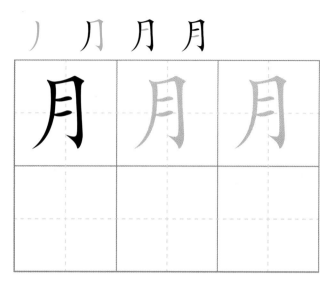

汉字小常识 Did you know?

Some characters have developed from pictures of people or things which give clues to their meanings.

Guess what these characters mean. Write the letters.

a 耳     b 人     c 燕

# 多元学习 Connections

## Cultures

1. Learn about the difference between the solar calendar and the Chinese lunar calendar.

> The solar calendar is based on the movement of the earth around the sun.

> The Chinese lunar calendar is based on the cycles of the lunar phases.

2. Use paper plates to show phases of the moon.

一月 …… 十二月十五

# Project

1. Make your own calendar.

2. Play a guessing game. Say the dates of the festivals your friends show.

十月三十一日！

1 Follow the instruction on each gate to meet the beautiful Chang'e in the moon palace.

Write 'moon' in Chinese.

Say the password 279613 in Chinese.

Say your birthday in Chinese.

Say '15 August' in Chinese.

Read the month.

十一月

**2** Work with your friend. Colour the stars and the chillies.

| Words | 说 | 读 | 写 |
|---|---|---|---|
| 一月 | ☆ | ☆ | ☆ |
| 二月 | ☆ | ☆ | ☆ |
| 三月 | ☆ | ☆ | ☆ |
| 四月 | ☆ | ☆ | 🌶 |
| 五月 | ☆ | ☆ | 🌶 |
| 六月 | ☆ | ☆ | ☆ |
| 七月 | ☆ | ☆ | 🌶 |
| 八月 | ☆ | ☆ | ☆ |
| 九月 | ☆ | ☆ | 🌶 |
| 十月 | ☆ | ☆ | ☆ |
| 十一月 | ☆ | ☆ | ☆ |
| 十二月 | ☆ | ☆ | ☆ |

| Words and sentences | 说 | 读 | 写 |
|---|---|---|---|
| 月 | ☆ | ☆ | ☆ |
| 日 | ☆ | ☆ | ☆ |
| 燕子 | ☆ | 🌶 | 🌶 |
| 来 | ☆ | 🌶 | 🌶 |
| 回来 | ☆ | 🌶 | 🌶 |
| 四月四日，燕子来我们家了。 | ☆ | 🌶 | 🌶 |

| | |
|---|---|
| Say the months and dates | ☆ |
| Count from one to 31 | ☆ |

**3** What does your teacher say?

My teacher says ...

分享 Sharing

## Words I remember

| | | | | | |
|---|---|---|---|---|---|
| 一月 | yī yuè | January | 十月 | shí yuè | |
| 二月 | èr yuè | February | 十一月 | shí yī yu | |
| 三月 | sān yuè | March | 十二月 | shí èr yu | |
| 四月 | sì yuè | April | 月 | yuè | |
| 五月 | wǔ yuè | May | 日 | rì | |
| 六月 | liù yuè | June | 燕子 | yàn zi | |
| 七月 | qī yuè | July | 来 | lái | |
| 八月 | bā yuè | August | 回来 | huí lái | |
| 九月 | jiǔ yuè | September | | | |

October

November

December

month, moon

date, day

swallow

to come

to come back

# Other words

| 这 | | zhè | this |
| 家 | | jiā | home |
| 学 | 会 | xué huì | to have learned |
| 飞 | | fēi | to fly |
| 明 | 年 | míng nián | next year |
| 快 | | kuài | hurry, soon |
| 又 | | yòu | again |
| 到 | | dào | to come, to arrive |
| 了 | | le | (modal particle to indicate a change of status) |

# OXFORD
## UNIVERSITY PRESS

Oxford University Press is a department of the University of Oxford.
It furthers the University's objective of excellence in research, scholarship,
and education by publishing worldwide. Oxford is a registered trade mark of
Oxford University Press in the UK and in certain other countries

Published in Hong Kong by
Oxford University Press (China) Limited
39th Floor, One Kowloon, 1 Wang Yuen Street, Kowloon Bay,
Hong Kong

Illustrated by Anne Lee and Wildman

Photographs for reproduction permitted by Dreamstime.com

China National Publications Import & Export (Group) Corporation is an authorized distributor of
Oxford Elementary Chinese.

Please contact content@cnpiec.com.cn or 86-10-65856782

ISBN: 978-0-19-082141-8

10 9 8 7 6 5 4 3 2